[College Edition]

The Guide to
Low-Risk Drinking

by Randy Haveson, M.A.

Published by:

RISE Publishing

www.risespeaker.com

ISBN: 978-0692645970

Second Edition

Printed in the United States

Table of Contents

Dedication

I wouldn't be here if it weren't for the support, love, and (sometimes) kick in the behind from a few amazing and inspiring people. So this book is dedicated to Charlie, Leon, Phil W., and the nameless, faceless woman who volunteered her time and answered my call to the hotline at 1:30 a.m. on May 16, 1984. I also dedicate this to my parents, who have been there for me through the entire journey and continue to support me through thick and thin. To Jill, my wife, the string to my balloon. And finally, to Eden, my shining star. You inspire me to be a better person and a better father every day.

Introduction: Know the Code

This is a book that's long overdue. Finally, here is a proven, practical way to drink and lower your risk for problems. Up until now, there have been two primary messages when it comes to drinking alcohol. One is "just say no," but for three out of every four college students, this is not an option because they choose to drink. The only other message out there is to "drink responsibly." But what does that mean? If you ask five random college students to define responsible drinking, you will most likely get five completely different answers. The term is invalid because it has so many different definitions.

This book offers some solid, actionable guidelines for you to follow in order to keep you safe, healthy, and out of trouble when you choose to drink. Basically, this book is going to teach you *how* to drink!

There are low-risk guidelines you can follow when it comes to drinking, similar to the guidelines you're taught when it comes to safe driving. No one handed you the keys to a car and said, "Drive responsibly." We were taught the rules of the road. We were taught about the different signs on the road and what they mean. We drove with experienced drivers to learn how to drive safely. We learned about speed limits in different areas, when to brake and accelerate, and—most of all—how to lower our risk for putting ourselves and others in danger. Of course, there's always some risk when we drive, but there are ways to lower our risk.

Let's look at speed limits, for example. When we follow the speed limit, our chance of getting a ticket or being involved in a crash is low. The more we go over the speed limit, the more we put ourselves and those around us at risk. And, if we consistently go 15 to 20 mph over the speed limit or more, sooner or later there will most likely be a negative consequence.

The same is true of drinking. When you drink and exceed the low-risk guidelines, you're making a choice that increases your risk of putting yourself and those around you in danger, even in one night of drinking.

So, here we go. Here's the code for successful drinking, and it's as simple as 0-1-2-3. And even if you don't follow these guidelines all of the time, at least now you'll know what they are.

"Always do sober what you said you'd do drunk. That will teach you to keep your mouth shut."

— Ernest Hemingway

As Simple as 0-1-2-3

When it comes to drinking, all you have to do is pay attention to the code—a few simple numbers. There's nothing complicated about these guidelines. And you can ignore these numbers or pretend they don't matter, but when you don't play by these guidelines, you're choosing to increase your risk. The more you increase your risk, the more likely you are to experience unpleasant results. Think back to the earlier analogy. You might not agree with the speed limit in a certain area, but that doesn't mean you can ignore the speed limit without some measure of increased risk.

This formula is not random. I have spent years researching and developing a way to teach people how to be safer when it comes to drinking. These numbers are facts. The Core Institute is a small, five-person department within the Southern Illinois University Carbondale Student Health Center that conducts studies of college students nationally, using proven scientific methods. Student life departments then use the data to design programming to benefit students' health and well-being across the nation. To date, the Core Institute has the largest database on alcohol and other drug use of any post-secondary educational institution. The research for this book comes from their data.

Actual students, all around the country, report time after time that alcohol gets them into trouble when they don't follow the "zero, one, two, three" plan.

If you do choose to drink in a high-risk way—that is to say, without following the guidelines laid out in the next few pages—it would be a good idea to try and apply these guidelines to your party plan twice a year for a month at a time. That way, you'll know if you still have control over your drinking or if your drinking has control over you.

Let's draw a clear line in the sand. If you can follow these guidelines on a consistent basis, the chances of having an alcohol problem are slim. On the other hand, if you do your best to follow the guidelines and can't do it, it means you have an alcohol problem.

"I've created a new drink! I'm calling it the Piñata Colada! It's sweet and tasty, but when you wake up the next morning your head feels like it's been hitten with a stick [sic]."

— *José N. Harris*

Here are the guidelines, spelled out in an easy and concise way. And yes, it's as simple as 0-1-2-3!

ZERO is your limit if:

- ✓ You are driving

- ✓ You are on medication*

- ✓ You haven't eaten recently**

- ✓ You have a test, presentation, job interview, or something to do the next day that requires your full cognitive abilities

- ✓ You have been sick

- ✓ You are pregnant

- ✓ You are an alcoholic or a drug addict

- ✓ You have a gut feeling that drinking isn't a good idea right now

- ✓ You consistently have a bad reaction to alcohol (blackouts, passing out, throwing up)

✓ You have experienced symptoms of withdrawal when you stopped drinking in the past

*Alcohol interacts with many prescription and over-the-counter drugs, with unpredictable results. When combined with medications, even just a little alcohol can make you drowsy, uncoordinated, nauseated, or confused.

**It's important to note that foods with protein help absorb alcohol in your system. Eating carbs only would result in a higher alcohol content in your body. Eating pizza or snack foods does not constitute eating a meal. And eating salty foods can make you thirstier, which will make you want to drink more.

ZERO is also your limit if you're under 21. When you are under the legal age for drinking, you put yourself at risk with *any* alcohol use. Think of it this way: You're over 21 and go to dinner with friends. At dinner, you have a few drinks and, on the way home, you're pulled over and asked to take a breathalyzer test. You blow a .04. Being over 21, nothing happens. However, if you're under 21 and blow a .04, you are eligible for what's called an "underage DUI." This is much worse than a regular DUI and it stays on your record for up to 10 years. If you plan to attend grad school, medical school, or law school, you will have to disclose any felonies on your record and an underage DUI conviction is a felony.

There are hundreds more reasons to make ZERO your number. Use your head and trust your instincts!

ONE is your limit in any 60-minute time frame.

A standard drink equals one twelve-ounce beer OR five ounces of wine OR one ounce of liquor.

One drink per hour is the low-risk guideline, simply because your liver can't handle any more than that at any given time. Think of it this way: you have the first drink and it goes to your liver for processing. You have a second drink in the first hour and your liver is still working on the first drink. So, the alcohol cruises through your blood stream, looking for somewhere else to go. It goes to your brain and it creates a little buzz. If you have a third drink in the first hour, your liver turns it away because it's still working on drink number one. It goes into your bloodstream, ends up in your brain, and now you are impaired. Your coordination might be off, your speech might become slurred, and you might think you're in control but, at this point, you're at a higher risk for problems.

Keep in mind that your liver is only able to metabolize one ounce of alcohol per hour, so that's why one drink per hour is the low-risk guideline.

Putting alcohol into your body, without giving the liver enough time to process it, puts a great strain on your liver. If your liver had nerve endings, drinking too much would be incredibly painful, as if it were on fire. Just like working out for too long in the gym can be painful.

Can you work out for six, eight, or ten hours in a row? When you have six, eight, or ten drinks, your liver has to work that many hours to break down the alcohol and process the ingredients.

TWO nights (or days) of drinking is your limit in any given week.

Studies from the Core Institute show that people who get in trouble with alcohol tend to drink three or more nights per week. By "trouble," we mean more fights, a lower GPA, and more classes missed than those drinking two times or less per week, to name a few. So, to drink in a low-risk way, you need to avoid drinking more than twice a week.

This number is also a handy tool to see if it's possible to limit your drinking: do you control your alcohol intake or does alcohol control you?

Are you in control of the alcohol or is the alcohol in control of you?

THREE drinks is your limit in any 24-hour period.

Yes, three. I know some of you are thinking, "Three!? Are you serious? If I only have three, then why bother?" And others are thinking, "Three!? Do I have to have that much?" Again, what we're talking about are low-risk guidelines. Up until now, there haven't been any guidelines. This is like putting a new speed limit sign on a highway that didn't have a speed limit before. Some people may think, "What is that about?! I don't want to drive that slowly," while others may think, "Thank goodness! Finally, I won't be so scared driving on this road anymore." Your behavior and your experience dictate your perspective. This book is meant to give you a new perspective—one that will help you make better decisions when it comes to drinking. Each year, too many people hurt themselves or others. It's time we finally had a speed limit for drinking.

Statistically, students who drink more than three drinks in a day (or night) are more likely to have trouble with police, residence halls, and other campus authorities. They also tend to miss more classes, have lower GPAs, and lower graduation rates. Less harmful, but more commonly associated consequences of frequent drinking are things like having a hangover, doing something you later regret, getting into an argument or fight, missing a class, getting criticized by someone you know, memory loss, nausea, or vomiting.

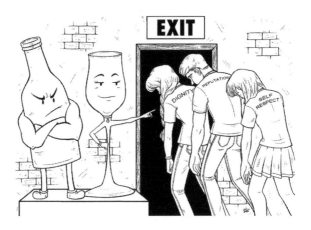

Don't let one night of drinking cause you to lose your dignity, self-respect, or reputation. A reputation is easy to form, but difficult to change.

Don't forget: each drink should be no more than a 12-ounce beer OR a 5-ounce glass of wine OR a 1-ounce serving of liquor. Everclear, moonshine, and other concoctions with high alcohol content ("proof" number) are much stronger and more toxic than typical liquor and should be avoided to minimize your risks while drinking.

It is important to note that the low- risk guidelines laid out in this book are simply that—"guidelines." There is always risk involved in drinking because so many factors come into play. For example, for those of a petite stature or with a low tolerance, three in an evening or even one per hour can put them at risk. Following these guidelines does not guarantee you won't have alcohol related problems; it just lowers your risk for problems. Think of it this way: the only way to guarantee you don't drown is to not get in the pool. Sure, you can learn to swim, wear a life vest, or use other precautions to lower your risk of drowning, but the only way to guarantee not drowning is to not get in the pool in the first place.

Fun Fact: Students with an A average generally have 3.6 drinks a week, C students average 9.5 drinks a week, and D and F students consume almost 18 drinks a week.

Party with a Plan®

No one plans to get hurt, start an argument, injure others, end up in jail, or experience any other bad situations after a night of partying. If you start off with a plan, it's more likely that you and those around you will stay safe.

Every year, at colleges around the country, there are 1,800 deaths and 250,000 injuries linked to alcohol use. The sad part is that all of these deaths and injuries are 100% avoidable. By following these guidelines, we can drastically reduce these numbers—starting now.

When you drink, remember that your actions have consequences—not just for you, but for everyone you come in contact with.

In order to be low-risk, ask yourself these questions before you go out:

WHO are you going out with? Who are you meeting later on? It's important to stick to your plan and come home with the same people you went out with. Those who get in trouble are usually those who alter their plan later in the evening, after they have exceeded the low-risk guidelines. And if "that guy" or "that gal" is really special, a date the next night is much safer than altering your plan for a hookup that same night.

WHAT are you planning to do? Are you planning to include alcohol? Do you have the details in mind before you leave your room or apartment? Again, stick to your plan. Sure, things can change as the night goes on, but evaluate changes and whether or not they increase your risk for trouble.

WHERE are you going? Make sure you have a plan and stick to it. If you're going somewhere alone, make sure others know where you're going and when you plan to be there. The more you plan, the safer you will be.

WHEN Know your limit (your "when") and stick to it. The majority of people who get in trouble with alcohol go over their limit or didn't have a plan to begin with. Thinking, "I'm just going to get drunk," is very dangerous because the person plans to drink without any limits at all. This is actually the way I used to drink, and that's one of the reasons I became an alcoholic. Obviously, this kind of thinking proved extremely unwise in my life, and sadly this has been the case for many others, too.

WHY are you drinking? Are you blowing off steam, looking to relax, or drinking to escape? Knowing why you're drinking can help you avoid trouble and additional problems. Treating alcohol as a way to escape can lead to additional problems, like state-dependent learning. This means that if you get into the habit of drinking for a certain reason, you start to think that the only time you can do that is when you drink. A good example is dancing. Many people feel like they can't dance unless they are drunk. This is state-dependent learning. And it's just not true. Your ability to dance is not inside a glass of alcohol; it's inside of you! So if you drink to reduce stress, lower anxiety, or to become more social, you're setting up a mechanism in your brain that thinks that the only way you can do these things is if you use alcohol.

HOW are you getting home? Know this before you go out! Is your driver planning to drink? If so, make sure you have an alternate ride home.

Fun Fact: The Romans first developed drinking games around 300 BC. I guess togas and beer pong aren't just a fraternity thing.

"I went out with a guy who once told me I didn't need to drink to make myself more fun to be around. I told him, I'm drinking so that you're more fun to be around."

— Chelsea Handler, *Are You There, Vodka? It's Me, Chelsea*

What about Drugs Other than Alcohol?

People ask me all the time about low-risk use of drugs other than alcohol. There's even the myth for some that marijuana is safer to use than alcohol. And it's just not true. Here are the facts: drugs other than alcohol (including prescription drugs not prescribed specifically for you) can't be used without risk. It's possible to use alcohol in a low-risk way because following these guidelines means you're not drinking to the point of intoxication. It's when people become intoxicated that risk begins to occur.

The main reason people use drugs other than alcohol is to become intoxicated. They use drugs to get high. If they didn't get high, they wouldn't use the drug. I've heard many marijuana smokers attempt to talk themselves into believing they are low-risk users, but it's just not possible. It's impossible to use drugs in a low-risk way. Any use of marijuana or drugs (other than alcohol) is high risk because there's no way to use the drug without becoming impaired. And, speaking of marijuana, there's no way to evaluate what the effect of the drug is going to be. If two people share a joint, one person might feel a slight buzz, while another is completely impaired. One person might have a great experience, while another has hallucinations and paranoia.

Is marijuana safer than alcohol? The answer is no. Most people compare the use of marijuana with the abuse of alcohol, and this is not a fair comparison. If alcohol is used according to the low-risk guidelines, then alcohol is definitely safer than marijuana because two drinks in two hours, spaced an hour apart, is safer—with less impairment—than using the same amount of marijuana in the same time period.

Fun Fact: Rum originated on the island of Barbados in the 17th century. No wonder pirates never wanted to leave the Caribbean!

"To alcohol! The cause of... and solution to... all of life's problems."

— Matt Groening

It's All About the Brain

Our brains are programmed to reward behavior that sustains life and provides pleasure. That's why things like sex, chocolate, rollercoasters, and music are so pleasurable. "Feel-good" neurochemicals (such as norepinephrine, dopamine, and serotonin) are naturally produced, transmitted, and reused by our brains when we consume certain foods or engage in certain behaviors.

Alcohol and many other drugs trick our brains into functioning as if there are more of these feel-good chemicals at work in our system than there actually are. As a result, our brain begins to slow down the natural production and/or re-use of these chemicals, and we need a little more alcohol, or another substance, each time in order to feel "normal."

For people who become accustomed to drinking in a high-risk way, it becomes a vicious cycle. The loss of your natural ability to experience pleasure increases your craving for whatever substance can help you return to "normal." This alters your brain's chemical balance even further, until everything is out of whack and you feel really crummy almost all the time when you're not using or drinking.

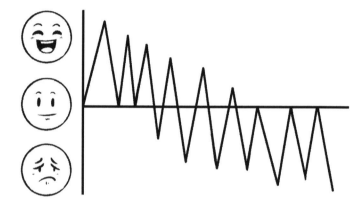

At first there's a high involved with using alcohol in a high-risk way. After a while though, a tolerance can develop and a pattern can start to form where the person starts to "need" alcohol just to feel normal. When they're not drinking, they can feel sad and depressed.

Once the cycle is broken, you have to "retrain" your brain. It will take a while—sometimes weeks or months—before someone who is alcohol dependent (dependent on alcohol to have fun or even function) starts to feel pleasure again without the use of chemicals.

This is why relapse is so prevalent for people attempting to get sober. The natural feel-good chemical factory closes down, so people feel depressed when they're not getting high or drunk. And it takes a while for the natural factory to fire itself up again. This is why it's important for newly sober people to find a support group of other sober people, so they can be assured that what they're feeling is normal and that it will pass.

Fun Fact: Rum originated on the island of Barbados in the 17th century. No wonder pirates never wanted to leave the Caribbean!

"First you take a drink, then the drink takes a drink, then the drink takes you."

— *F. Scott Fitzgerald*

When You Assume...

Over the years, I've heard so many myths and fallacies about alcohol and other drugs. People tend to believe whatever they want to believe and whatever the common thought is within their peer group. Here are some of the most common:

"Everybody drinks, right?" Actually, only three out of every four college students drink alcohol. That means almost 25% of all college students don't drink at all! And yes, they're having fun... without the hangover! Attend that next party sober and remind yourself that alcohol isn't necessary to have a good time.

"It's awkward going to a party and not drinking like everybody else." Yes, it can be. Depending on what's comfortable for you, you can say you're on medication that interacts poorly with

alcohol. Or just say you don't feel like drinking. Or carry around a red cup with water in it. Remember, one out of every four students doesn't drink. You're not alone! And a true friend will support your decision to not drink. There's a difference between a friend and a drinking buddy. A friend supports you and your healthy decisions. A drinking buddy needs company and will pressure you to drink with him or her.

"My life is so stressful; I have to let off steam somehow." If you use alcohol or drugs to relax, manage stress, deal with anxiety or other overwhelming emotional issues, you're depriving your brain of the natural feel-good chemicals it needs. You will need an ever-increasing amount of artificial substances to mimic that natural effect. This is called *tolerance* and it's one of the signs of alcoholism.

Alcohol tolerance creates a downward spiral that usually ends badly one way or another. If you're struggling with stress or emotional problems, **ask for help**. Student health services are readily available, and your confidentiality is guaranteed by law. You can ask for help online, anonymously, or you can call a crisis hotline in your area. Asking for help is not a weakness; rather it demonstrates that you have courage, strength, and common sense.

Fun Fact: A Chinese imperial edict from around 1116 BCE claimed that a moderate consumption of alcohol was a religious obligation.

"I always take Scotch whiskey at night as a preventive of toothache. I have never had the toothache; and what is more, I never intend to have it."

— Mark Twain

How to Have Fun without Alcohol

Ask one of the 25% of college students *who don't drink* how they hang out and have fun. You might get some answers like these:

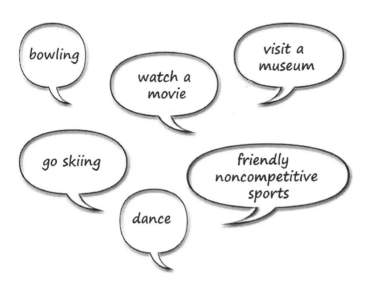

Fun Fact: While ancient Romans frowned on drunken behavior, by 200 BC it was much more prevalent. By 50 BC drunkenness was out of control and some say alcohol misuse could have been one of the reasons for the fall of the Roman Empire. Maybe it was all those drinking games.

"I drink too much. The last time I gave a urine sample, it had an olive in it."

— Rodney Dangerfield

"When you stop drinking, you have to deal with this marvelous personality that started you drinking in the first place."

— Jimmy Breslin

The Challenge and Summary

I talk to adults all the time who tell me they wish they had had these guidelines when they were in college. To be honest, I wish I would have had them too. If I had been given solid guidelines to follow and was more conscious about the choices I made in regard to alcohol, maybe I wouldn't have become an alcoholic. But I'll never know. The whole purpose of this book is to help you make better choices and become more conscious of your drinking habits.

My challenge is this: if you are one of the 35% of students who consistently make high-risk choices, every six months or so try pulling back and follow the low-risk guidelines for a month. See if you still have control. Even better, do this: to really see if you're in control of alcohol or if alcohol is in control of you, go 30 days without *any* alcohol or other drugs. I say "other drugs" because there are some who would stop drinking but increase their marijuana use. Substituting one drug for another does not show controlled use. I call this "changing seats on the Titanic." For those who do have a problem with alcohol or other drugs, it doesn't matter which drug you're doing; you just need to do a drug, and any of them will bring you down. So, quit for 30 days. See if you go through any type of withdrawal. See if you can have fun without drinking. See what happens to your grades, your class attendance, and your ability to study. And most of all, see if your alcohol use has turned to dependence or addiction.

Alcohol can be cunning. It might seem like the solution when it is actually the problem. No one plans to become an alcoholic. No one plans to have one night of drinking change his or her entire life. But it happens all the time. I've watched some really good people hurt themselves and others because of one bad decision. If you find you do have a problem, or know someone else who has a problem, seek help! Yes, there's still a huge stigma associated with addiction, but that is changing. There are people on your campus and in your community who can help. The resources at the end of this book are there to help you.

Fun Fact: The first form of tequila was made by the Aztecs in 1000 BC. The Cuervo family introduced distilled tequila in 1758.

"Ignorance is a lot like alcohol: the more you have of it, the less you are able to see its effect on you."

— Jay M. Bylsma

To Parents

I talk to many parents who are terrified when they think about their children going off to college. They hear the horror stories of college drinking and think, "What if that happens to my kid?" Keep in mind that the stories you hear on the news are sensationalized. These are the out-of-the-ordinary stories. Yes, 1,800 college students die from alcohol or drugs every year. But 6,998,200 don't. You will never hear on the news, "Dorm room full of college students watched movies and laughed until 3:00 in the morning. No one drank alcohol or used drugs. Details at 11!" If you are the parent of a college student, here are some tips you can use to assist your child in making good decisions around alcohol in college:

- Talk to them. Have an honest discussion about your fears and how you want them to make good decisions, especially around alcohol. Discuss the low-risk guidelines and ask them if they make sense.

- Discuss how alcohol is the fuel for most other problems that can occur. Let them know that 75% of all sexual assaults happen when one or both people are under the influence. Most fights, accidents, and car wrecks happen when someone is under the influence.

- Talk about their goals and dreams for college and discuss what might get in their way. Talk about how to lower their risk for problems or detours.

- If you used or drank in college, don't glamorize your use or experiences. The more you present high-risk choices as acceptable or even desirable, the more likely your children are to move in that direction. Keep in mind that it is a different world today. Drugs are more powerful, consequences are more severe, and the pressure students are under today can be overwhelming.

- Don't drink with them. Many parents feel like they need to normalize drinking by drinking with their child. Big mistake. You've just reinforced that drinking under age is okay. They will reason that if it's okay to drink with you, then it's going to be okay to drink with their friends later on.

- If you see signs that there's a problem, don't ignore it. Many parents think, "Maybe the problem will go away or solve itself." Most of the time, it doesn't. If you notice a change in behavior, a change in friends, falling grades, or a new apathy, look for help or support. Most campuses have counseling centers. Some now have campus social workers who help students who are showing signs of a problem. There are many off-campus resources you can use. Some of them are listed in the following pages.

Fun Fact: Not only did the Chinese invent spaghetti, it looks like they also invented wine. The oldest known wine remnants were found on pottery shards dating back to 7000 BC. So think fondly of the Chinese as you eat your spaghetti and drink your red wine.

"One reason I don't drink is that I want to know when I am having a good time."

— Nancy Astor

Further Reading and Resources

I get most of my statistics about drinking behaviors from the Core Institute, which maintains the largest national database about college students' drinking and drug use in the United States. Explore their website at http://core.siu.edu/index.html

Another reliable, comprehensive resource: National Institute on Alcohol Abuse and Alcoholism http://niaaa.nih.gov/

On drugs and drug abuse: www.drugabuse.gov

On exercise and brain chemistry: http://www.livestrong.com/article/320144-does-exercise-release-a-chemical-in-the-brain/

For information on treatment programs:
http://www.collegetreatment.com

Recovery resources for college students:
http://www.transformingyouthrecovery.org and
http://collegiaterecovery.org

Alcoholics Anonymous: http://www.aa.org

Narcotics Anonymous: https://www.na.org

Cocaine Anonymous: http://www.ca.org

Does someone else's drinking bother you?
Al-Anon can help: http://www.al-anon.org

Think you might have a problem with alcohol?
Visit the National Council on Alcoholism and Drug
Dependence:
https://ncadd.org/learn-about-alcohol/alcohol-
abuse-self-test

About the Author:
Randy Haveson

Randy has been working in the addiction field since 1986 and in higher education since 1990. He has a BA in Psychology, an MA in Counseling, and he jokes that he has a PhD in personal experience. His warm demeanor, keen sense of humor, and powerful message makes him one of the best and most sought-after speakers on the college market today. He was named one of the "Best of the Best" speakers by the BACCHUS Network at their 25-year-anniversary celebration and was honored by the Georgia chapter of the National Speaker's Association by being named the Showcase Speaker of the Year in 2002.

In 2014, Randy founded RISE Speaking & Consulting, founded on the four pillars of Recovery, Intervention, Support, and Education. He works from the heart, and his mission is to help keep others from falling into the pit of addiction and assisting those who have. For more information about Randy and his speaking, training, and consulting opportunities, visit RISE at www.risespeaker.com.

"Drink provokes the desire, but it takes away the performance."

— *William Shakespeare, Macbeth*

"Alcohol ruined me financially and morally, broke my heart and the hearts of too many others. Even though it did this to me and it almost killed me and I haven't touched a drop of it in seventeen years, sometimes I wonder if I could get away with drinking some now. I totally subscribe to the notion that alcoholism is a mental illness because thinking like that is clearly insane."

— Craig Ferguson, *American on Purpose: The Improbable Adventures of an Unlikely Patriot*

Final Thoughts

When I was growing up, no one ever taught me how to drink. The information I received about alcohol and other drugs was that it was cool. It was fun. It was a way to feel more relaxed and out of your own head. I was scared the first time I drank, but I did it anyway, and I loved it. I also felt the same way about pot, cocaine, and hallucinogens. I hung out with people who drank and used like I did. There weren't any guidelines. No one ever stood up and said, "Whoa, dude, you need to slow down."

For a while, I was having fun, but, just like the graph showed, the fun slowed down and the dependency began. I thought alcohol was the solution when it was actually the problem. By the time I was 21, I was a full-blown addict, but I didn't stop until I was 24. I went through hell. I put my family though hell. I became a person I never wanted to be, so I decided to write this book for the hundreds of thousands of people out there who are on the same path that I was on. I'm hoping that it doesn't have to get as bad for you as it did for me. I thought that by writing some guidelines, I might help people make better decisions than I did.

It's funny though, when you think about it. I'm an alcoholic that teaches people how to drink. But hey, who better than an alcoholic to teach people how to drink? I realize now that I don't need a glass of alcohol to dance, a joint to be creative, or a line to be charming, witty, and funny. All of those qualities are inside of ME, not in other substances. Today I'm happy, my life is full, and I don't drink or use. There's no shame in asking for help. I did, back in 1984, and it saved my life. Now I get to be here, writing these words for you. Who knows what kind of greatness is inside of you, waiting to get out? So, go find out. And don't let something like alcohol or other drugs get in your way. You are a product of the choices you make, so make good choices.

NOTES

45309866R00039

Made in the USA
San Bernardino, CA
05 February 2017